Hot Math Topics

Problem Solving, Communication, and Reasoning

Number Sense and Computation

grade **3**

Carole Greenes
Linda Schulman Dacey
Rika Spungin

Dale Seymour Publications®
White Plains, New York

DALE SEYMOUR PUBLICATIONS®

This book is published by Dale Seymour Publications®,
an imprint of Addison Wesley Longman, Inc.

Dale Seymour Publications
10 Bank Street
White Plains, New York 10602
Customer Service: 800-872-1100

Managing Editor: Catherine Anderson
Senior Editor: John Nelson
Project Editor: Mali Apple
Production/Manufacturing Director: Janet Yearian
Sr. Production/Manufacturing Coordinator: Fiona Santoianni
Design Director: Phyllis Aycock
Cover and Interior Illustrations: Jared Lee
Text and Cover Design: Tracey Munz
Composition and Computer Graphics: Alan Noyes

Copyright © 1999 by Addison Wesley Longman, Inc. All rights reserved.
Printed in the United States of America.

The publisher grants permission to individual teachers who have purchased this book to
reproduce the blackline masters as needed for use with their own students. Reproduction
for an entire school or school district or for commercial use is prohibited.

Order number 21874
ISBN 0-7690-0016-9

1 2 3 4 5 6 7 8 9 10-ML-03 02 01 00 99

Contents

Introduction

Why Was *Hot Math Topics* Developed?

The *Hot Math Topics* series was developed for several reasons:

- to offer students practice and maintenance of previously learned skills and concepts
- to enhance problem solving and mathematical reasoning abilities
- to build literacy skills
- to nurture collaborative learning behaviors

Practicing and maintaining concepts and skills

Although textbooks and core curriculum materials do treat the topics explored in this series, their treatment is often limited by the lesson format and the page size. As a consequence, there are often not enough opportunities for students to practice newly acquired concepts and skills related to the topics, or to connect the topics to other content areas. *Hot Math Topics* provides the necessary practice and mathematical connections.

Similarly, core instructional programs often do not do a very good job of helping students maintain their skills. Although textbooks do include reviews of previously learned material, they are frequently limited to sidebars or boxed-off areas on one or two pages in each chapter, with four or five exercises in each box. Each set of problems is intended only as a sampling of previously taught topics, rather than as a complete review. In the selection and placement of the review exercises, little or no attention

is given to levels of complexity of the problems. By contrast, *Hot Math Topics* targets specific topics and gives students more experience with concepts and skills related to them. The problems are sequenced by difficulty, allowing students to hone their skills. And, because they are not tied to specific lessons, the problems can be used at any time.

Enhancing problem solving and mathematical reasoning abilities

Hot Math Topics presents students with situations in which they may use a variety of problem solving strategies, including

- designing and conducting experiments to generate or collect data
- guessing, checking, and revising guesses
- organizing data in lists or tables in order to identify patterns and relationships
- choosing appropriate computational algorithms and deciding on a sequence of computations
- using inverse operations in "work backward" solution paths

For their solutions, students are also required to bring to bear various methods of reasoning, including

- deductive reasoning
- inductive reasoning
- proportional reasoning

For example, to solve clue-type problems, students must reason deductively and make inferences about mathematical relationships in order to generate candidates for the solutions and to home in on those that meet all of the problem's conditions.

To identify and continue a pattern and then write a rule for finding the next term in that pattern, students must reason inductively.

To compute unit prices and make trades, students must reason proportionally.

In addition to using these reasoning methods, students must apply their number sense skills. Number sense is brought to bear when students estimate or compare magnitudes of numbers and when they must determine the type of number appropriate for a given situation.

Building communication and literacy skills

Hot Math Topics offers students opportunities to write and talk about mathematical ideas. For many problems, students must describe their solution paths, justify their solutions, give their opinions, or write or tell stories.

Some problems have multiple solution methods. With these problems, students may have to compare their methods with those of their peers and talk about how their approaches are alike and different.

Other problems have multiple solutions, requiring students to confer to be sure they have found all possible answers.

Nurturing collaborative learning behaviors

Several of the problems can be solved by students working together. Some are designed specifically as partner problems. By working collaboratively, students can develop expertise in posing questions that call for clarification or verification, brainstorming solution strategies, and following another person's line of reasoning.

What Is in *Number Sense and Computation?*

This book contains 100 problems and tasks that focus on number sense and operations. The mathematics content, the mathematical connections, the problem solving strategies, and the communication skills that are emphasized are described below.

Mathematics content

Number sense and operations problems and tasks require students to

- add or subtract with up to four-digit numbers
- multiply by single-digit multipliers
- divide by single-digit divisors
- compute with money
- identify place-value and numeration patterns
- order numbers and compare numbers of up to eight digits
- compute and compare unit prices
- round numbers to nearer ten or hundred
- interpret remainders
- estimate quantities, sums, differences, and products
- identify various ways numbers are used
- use number sense to match numbers to given situations
- find fractional parts of quantities and compare fractional parts of a whole

Mathematical connections

In these problems and tasks, connections are made to these other topic areas:

- algebra
- measurement
- geometry
- number theory
- graphs
- statistics

Problem solving strategies

Number Sense and Computation problems and tasks offer students opportunities to use one or more of several problem solving strategies.

- **Formulate Questions:** When data are presented in displays or text form, students must pose one or more questions that can be answered using the given data.

- **Complete Stories:** When confronted with an incomplete story, students must supply the missing information and then check that the story makes sense.

- **Organize Information:** To ensure that several solution candidates for a problem are considered, students may have to organize information by drawing a picture, making a list, or constructing a table.

- **Guess, Check, and Revise:** In some problems, students have to identify or generate candidates for the solution and then check whether those candidates match the conditions of the problem. If the conditions are not satisfied, other possible solutions must be generated and verified.

- **Identify and Continue Patterns:** To identify the next term or terms in a sequence, students have to recognize the relationship between successive terms and then generalize that relationship.

- **Use Logic:** Students have to reason deductively, from clues, to make inferences about the solution to a problem. They must reason proportionately to determine which of two buys is better. They have to reason inductively to continue patterns.

- **Work Backward:** In some problems, the output is given and students must determine the input by identifying mathematical relationships between the input and output and applying inverse operations.

Communication skills

Problems and tasks in *Number Sense and Computation* are designed to stimulate communication. As part of the solution process, students may have to

- describe their thinking steps
- find alternate solution methods and solution paths
- identify other possible answers
- formulate problems for classmates to solve
- compare estimates, solutions, and methods with classmates
- make drawings to clarify mathematical relationships

These communication skills are enhanced when students interact with one another and with the teacher. By communicating both orally and in writing, students develop their understanding and use of the language of mathematics.

How Can *Hot Math Topics* Be Used?

The problems may be used as practice of newly learned concepts and skills, as maintenance of previously learned ideas, and as enrichment experiences for early finishers or more advanced students.

They may be used in class or assigned for homework. If used during class, they may be selected to complement lessons dealing with a specific topic or assigned every week as a means of keeping skills alive and well. Because the problems often require the application of various problem solving strategies and reasoning methods, they may also form the basis of whole-class lessons whose goals are to develop expertise with specific problem solving strategies or methods.

The problems, which are sequenced from least to most difficult, may be used by students working in pairs or on their own. The selection of problems may be made by the teacher or the students based on their needs or interests. If the plan is for students to choose problems, you may wish to copy individual problems onto card stock and laminate them, and establish a problem card file.

To facilitate record keeping, a Management Chart is provided on page 6. The chart can be duplicated so that there is one for each student. As a problem is completed, the space corresponding to that problem's number may be shaded. An Award Certificate is included on page 6 as well.

How Can Student Performance Be Assessed?

Number Sense and Computation problems and tasks provide you with opportunities to assess students'

- number sense skills
- computation ability
- problem solving abilities
- mathematical reasoning methods
- communication skills

Observations

Keeping anecdotal records helps you to remember important information you gain as you observe students at work. To make observations more manageable, limit each observation to a group of from four to six students or to one of the areas noted above. You may find that using index cards facilitates the recording process.

Discussions

Many of the *Number Sense and Computation* problems and tasks allow for multiple answers or may be solved in a variety of ways. This built-in richness motivates students to discuss their work with one another. Small groups or class discussions are appropriate. As students share their approaches to the problems, you will gain additional insights into their content knowledge, mathematical reasoning, and communication abilities.

Scoring responses

You may wish to holistically score students' responses to the problems and tasks. The simple scoring rubric below uses three levels: high, medium, and low.

High	Medium	Low
• Solution demonstrates that the student knows the concepts and skills.	• Solution demonstrates that the student has some knowledge of the concepts and skills.	• Solution shows that the student has little or no grasp of the concepts and skills.
• Solution is complete and thorough.	• Solution is complete.	• Solution is incomplete or contains major errors.
• The student communicates effectively.	• The student communicates somewhat clearly.	• The student does not communicate effectively.

Portfolios

Having students store their responses to the problems in *Hot Math Topics* portfolios allows them to see improvement in their work over time. You may want to have them choose examples of their best responses for inclusion in their permanent portfolios, accompanied by explanations as to why each was chosen.

Students and the assessment process

Involving students in the assessment process is central to the development of their abilities to reflect on their own work, to understand the assessment standards to which they are held accountable, and to take ownership for their own learning. Young children may find the reflective process difficult, but with your coaching, they can develop such skills.

Discussion may be needed to help students better understand your standards for performance. Ask students such questions as, "What does it mean to communicate *clearly*?" "What is a *complete* response?" Some students may want to use a rubric to score their responses.

Participation in peer-assessment tasks will also help students to better understand the performance standards. In pairs or small groups, students can review each other's responses and offer feedback. Opportunities to revise work may then be given.

What Additional Materials Are Needed?

Calculators and newspapers are required for solving some of the problems in *Number Sense and Computation*. Other manipulatives and materials may be helpful, including base ten blocks, a hundred chart, play money, tiles of various shapes, and a digital clock. Rulers, scissors, and grid paper should be readily accessible.

Management Chart

Name _____

When a problem or task is completed, shade the box with that number.

1	2	3	4	5	6	7	8	9	10
11	12	13	14	15	16	17	18	19	20
21	22	23	24	25	26	27	28	29	30
31	32	33	34	35	36	37	38	39	40
41	42	43	44	45	46	47	48	49	50
51	52	53	54	55	56	57	58	59	60
61	62	63	64	65	66	67	68	69	70
71	72	73	74	75	76	77	78	79	80
81	82	83	84	85	86	87	88	89	90
91	92	93	94	95	96	97	98	99	100

Award Certificate

Hot Math Topics

SUPER SOLVER

this certifies that

_____

has been awarded the Hot Math Topics Super Solver Certificate for

Excellence in Problem Solving

_____   _____
date   signature

©Addison Wesley Longman, Inc./Published by Dale Seymour Publications®

Problems and Tasks

Darryl had some money in his pocket.

- He bought a kite for $9.
- He bought some string for $2.
- He has $4 left.

How much money did Darryl have at the start?

How did you solve the problem?

- -

Mia, June, and Ali played games at the fair.

They won tickets to get prizes.

The girls used all their tickets.

Mia got 2 prizes with her 13 tickets.

Mia got _____ and _____ .

June got 3 prizes with her 18 tickets.

June got _____ and _____ and _____ .

Make up a problem about Ali.

Tell the number of prizes and the number of tickets.

©Addison Wesley Longman, Inc./Published by Dale Seymour Publications®

©Addison Wesley Longman, Inc./Published by Dale Seymour Publications®

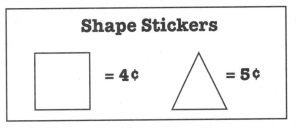

How much does this design cost?

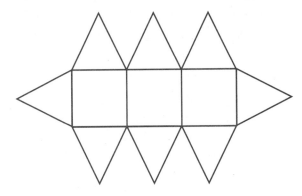

Draw a design that costs 50¢.

- -

©Addison Wesley Longman, Inc./Published by Dale Seymour Publications®

Craig spent $36. What did he buy?

Is there another answer?

How could you find the number of ❀ without counting every ❀?

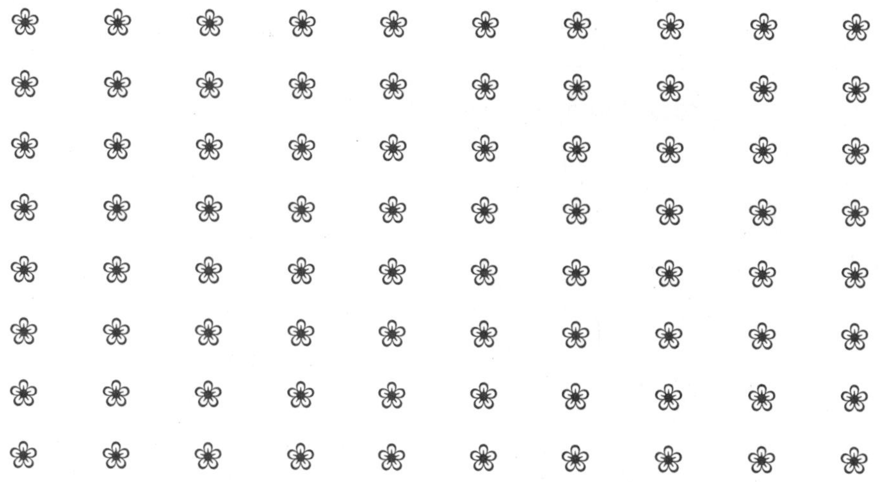

©Addison Wesley Longman, Inc./Published by Dale Seymour Publications®

(rows of ❀ flowers, 10 across and 8 down)

- -

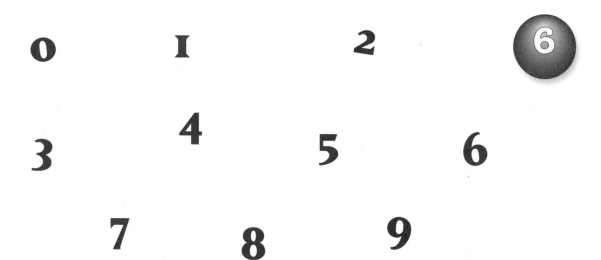

0   1   2

4
3   5   6

7   8   9

Put the numbers into two groups.

Tell how the numbers within each group are alike.

Compare your answer with a friend's.

©Addison Wesley Longman, Inc./Published by Dale Seymour Publications®

Work with a partner.

Make a list of places where there are numbers in your homes.

Tell how each type of number is used.

Numbers that tell how many or how much	Numbers that are measurements	Numbers that are labels

---

The shading and number patterns continue.

What numbers will be shaded in the bottom row?

1	2	3	4	5	6	7	8	9	10
11	12	13	14	15	16	17	18	19	20
21	22	23	24	25	26	27	28	29	30
31	32	33	34	35	36	37	38	39	40
41	42	43							

©Addison Wesley Longman, Inc./Published by Dale Seymour Publications®

©Addison Wesley Longman, Inc./Published by Dale Seymour Publications®

The graph shows the books the children read.
How many books were not about dinosaurs?
Tell how you found out.

©Addison Wesley Longman, Inc./Published by Dale Seymour Publications®

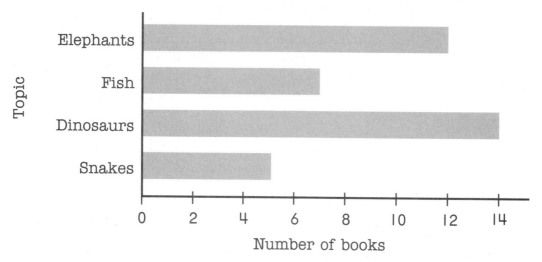

Science Books Read in Ms. Chou's Class

Topic / Number of books

(Elephants: 12, Fish: 7, Dinosaurs: 14, Snakes: 5)

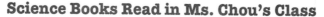

Jan, Nathan, and Kara made points on each of their 3 tosses.

- Jan said, "I got 24 points."
- Nathan said, "I got 23 points."
- Kara said, "I got 21 points."

One of them is not telling the truth.

Who is it? Tell how you know.

MAKE POINTS
WIN PRIZES

©Addison Wesley Longman, Inc./Published by Dale Seymour Publications®

11

Kai and Becky made some cookies.

They gave 5 cookies to Rosa.

They gave 3 cookies to Tia.

They gave 5 cookies to Ryan.

They were left with 4 cookies each.

How many cookies did Kai and Becky make?

12

Take a survey in your class.

Compare your class's favorite sports to this class's favorite sports.

Favorite Sports in Mr. Bond's Class

Sport	Number of students
baseball	
football	
gymnastics	
soccer	

⊼ = 2 students

Here are 5 ways to name 36.

$4 \times 8 + 4$

$72 \div 2$

$5 \times 7 + 1$

6×6

thirty-six

Find 3 other ways to name 36.

Compare your ways with those of a classmate.

- -

1   **2**   3   **4**   (14)

Use all of the numbers shown.

Use each number once.

Use any operations: addition, subtraction, multiplication, division.

$+$ $-$ $\times$ $\div$

Tell how to get 15.

Can you find another way?

©Addison Wesley Longman, Inc./Published by Dale Seymour Publications®

15

Jeff has 3 quarters.

Kiran has 20¢ more than Jeff.

Eric has 15¢ less than Kiran.

How much money does Eric have?

16

Write the names of the cities on the lines.

Use the road sign to help you decide.

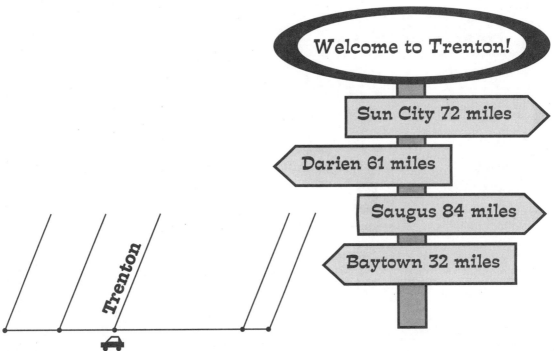

Welcome to Trenton!

Sun City 72 miles

Darien 61 miles

Saugus 84 miles

Baytown 32 miles

Trenton

©Addison Wesley Longman, Inc./Published by Dale Seymour Publications®

©Addison Wesley Longman, Inc./Published by Dale Seymour Publications®

Answer Sign

**50 6
7 27**

17

Use the facts.

Write a question for each answer on the Answer Sign.

Facts

- There are 15 girls and 9 boys in Everett's class.

- There are 8 girls and 18 boys in Niki's class.

- -

Here is part of a hundred chart.

Tell the value of A, B, C, and D.

18

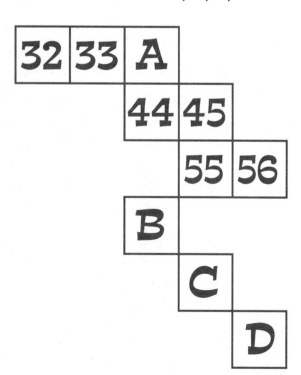

32	33	A
	44	45
		55	56
B
C
D

©Addison Wesley Longman, Inc./Published by Dale Seymour Publications®

When you add two numbers, you get 12.

When you subtract one of the numbers from the other, you get a number greater than 2.

Find all the pairs of numbers that work.

Fill in the blanks with numbers.

The story must make sense.

a. Barry has _____ baseball cards.

b. He has _____ football cards.

c. He has _____ more baseball than football cards.

d. He has _____ cards in all.

Which line—a, b, c, or d—will always have the greatest number?

©Addison Wesley Longman, Inc./Published by Dale Seymour Publications®

©Addison Wesley Longman, Inc./Published by Dale Seymour Publications®

2 $\frac{26}{3}$ $\frac{8}{10}$ 56

Use each number shown to complete the story.

Your story must make sense.

Daniel is _____ years old and is in grade _____ .

Daniel walks a total of _____ miles to and from school each day, or _____ miles each week.

There are _____ students in Daniel's class.

At _____ inches, Daniel is the tallest student in his class.

Which would you rather have?

Tell how you decided.

©Addison Wesley Longman, Inc./Published by Dale Seymour Publications®

©Addison Wesley Longman, Inc./Published by Dale Seymour Publications®

Fill in the blanks.

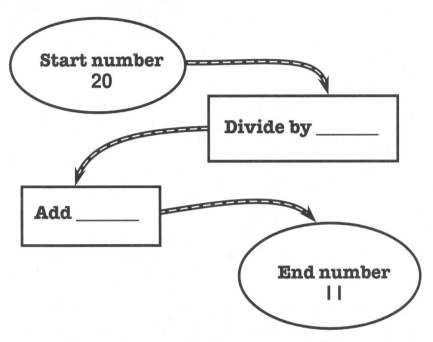

Start number
20

Divide by _____

Add _____

End number
11

Compare your flowchart with a classmate's.

- -

Ring two numbers in each box.

Their sum must be in the range.

©Addison Wesley Longman, Inc./Published by Dale Seymour Publications®

```
  13    8
        5
  39
     2
```
Range: 20–40

```
 15      17
    29
 7    32
```
Range: 50–100

```
 30   9
   59
 25  67
```
Range: 100–200

```
 390
     353
 220
     401
 200
```
Range: 300–500

$$\triangle + \square + \bigcirc = 16$$

$$\square + \bigcirc = 10$$

$$\square + \square = 16$$

$$\square = ? \qquad \bigcirc = ? \qquad \triangle = ?$$

- -

APPLES	45¢
RAISINS	40¢
NUTS	60¢
JUICE	80¢
MILK	75¢

Lucia bought a snack.

Her snack cost 5 quarters.

Simon bought a snack.

His snack cost 5 quarters.

Simon bought more items than Lucia bought.

What did each person buy?

©Addison Wesley Longman, Inc./Published by Dale Seymour Publications®

©Addison Wesley Longman, Inc./Published by Dale Seymour Publications®

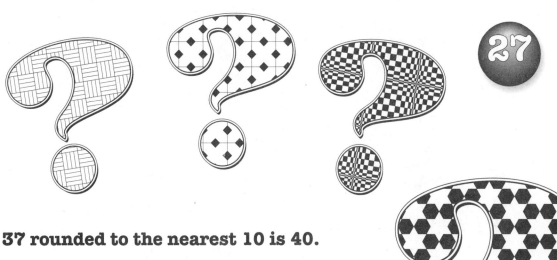

37 rounded to the nearest 10 is 40.

132 rounded to the nearest 10 is 130.

When you round a number to the nearest 10, do the number and the rounded number always have the same number of digits?

Explain.

Cary drove from Addtown to Subtract City.

He took the shortest route.

What route did Cary take?

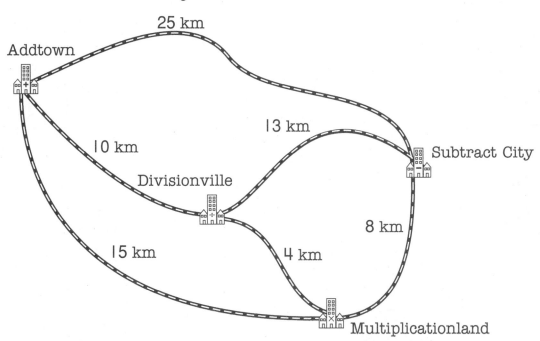

Which number is greater:

- the number of people in your city **or**
  the number of people in your state?

- the number of windows in your school **or**
  the number of telephones in your school?

- the number of days in a month **or**
  the number of Thursdays in a year?

Tell how you decided.

- -

Write a number in each blank.

The story must make sense.

Tami is ____ years old. She is in grade ____ .

Tami has ____ brothers.

Her older brother is ____ years old. He is
in grade ____ .

Her younger brother is ____ years old.

He is in grade ____ .

©Addison Wesley Longman, Inc./Published by Dale Seymour Publications®

©Addison Wesley Longman, Inc./Published by Dale Seymour Publications®

31

What is the cost of 6 pencils?

Tell two ways to find the answer.

©Addison Wesley Longman, Inc./Published by Dale Seymour Publications®

32

Don drove from Lakeville to Sandhill to Upton.

Then he drove from Upton to Sandhill.

How many miles did Don drive?

Make a drawing to help you solve the problem.

Each box holds 3 golf balls.

How many boxes are needed for 29 golf balls?

Tell how you decided.

- -

You are thinking of the number 18.

You want your friend to figure out your number with 4 clues.

Make up a fourth clue.

Clues

1. It is an even number less than 25.

2. It is a 2-digit number.

3. You do not say the number when you count by 5s.

4. _____

©Addison Wesley Longman, Inc./Published by Dale Seymour Publications®

©Addison Wesley Longman, Inc./Published by Dale Seymour Publications®

How can you use Problem A to help you fill
in the number in Problem B?

©Addison Wesley Longman, Inc./Published by Dale Seymour Publications®

Problem
A

Problem
B

$$
\begin{array}{r}
98 \\
+\ 30 \\
\hline
128
\end{array}
\qquad
\begin{array}{r}
98 \\
+\ \square \\
\hline
138
\end{array}
$$

Compare your ideas with a friend's ideas.

- -

Shirt $14.25   Jeans $23.50   Belt $9.98   Tie $10.50

David bought a shirt and a belt.

José bought a belt and a tie.

How much more did David spend than José?

Tell two ways to decide.

> I counted 48 wheels. I counted as many tricycle wheels as bicycle wheels.

The Cycle Shop sells bicycles and tricycles.

How many tricycles are there?

Write the steps you followed to solve the problem.

Find the length of each snake.

- The king cobra is about 3 times as long as the common cobra.

- Two thread snakes end to end are about 1 foot long.

- The water moccasin is about 2 feet shorter than the common cobra.

- The copperhead is about half the length of the water moccasin.

- The rattlesnake is 1 foot longer than the common cobra.

- The common cobra is about 6 feet long.

Snake Lengths

Snake	Length (feet)
Common cobra	
King cobra	
Copperhead	

Snake	Length (feet)
Rattlesnake	
Thread snake	
Water moccasin	

©Addison Wesley Longman, Inc./Published by Dale Seymour Publications®

©Addison Wesley Longman, Inc./Published by Dale Seymour Publications®

Write 3 math problems using the facts.

Facts

- Tomas and Dina collect Olympic stamps.

- Tomas has 7 pages of stamps with 6 stamps on each page.

- Dina has 5 pages of stamps with 8 stamps on each page.

Trade problems with a friend.

Solve your friend's problems.

You want to spend exactly 90¢.

What could you buy?

Make a list of the different ways to spend the money.

Suppose you number the pages of a book.

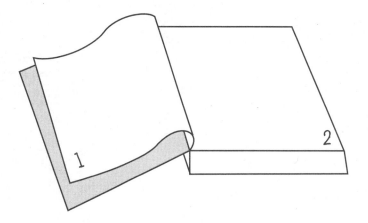

You get 1¢ for each one-digit number you write.

You get 2¢ for each two-digit number you write.

If you number the pages from 1 to 40, how much money will you get?

How much does a dozen cookies cost?

Tell two ways to find the answer.

©Addison Wesley Longman, Inc./Published by Dale Seymour Publications®

©Addison Wesley Longman, Inc./Published by Dale Seymour Publications®

Rhea has 7 coins. She has 56¢.

What are the coins?

Can you find three different sets of coins that work?

56¢

At Leoni's Pizza, you can order pizza with a thick or a thin crust.

You can order a cheese, a pepperoni, an onion, or a garlic pizza.

How many different pizzas can you order?

Make a list.

©Addison Wesley Longman, Inc./Published by Dale Seymour Publications®

2 pounds

3 pounds

4 pounds

5 pounds

7 pounds

9 pounds

You want to make the scale balance.

Fill in the weights with the number of pounds.

Use each number only once.

GREEN BEANS
SPECIAL!

BUY I CAN.
GET I CAN FREE!
60¢ PER CAN

GREEN
BEANS

Ms. Brook bought 8 cans of green beans.

How much did she pay?

Tell how you know.

©Addison Wesley Longman, Inc./Published by Dale Seymour Publications®

What number am I?

- I am greater than 20 + 19.

- I am less than 69 − 18.

- My ones digit is twice my tens digit.

- -

Complete the grid.

Add 20 going across.

Add 70 going up.

48

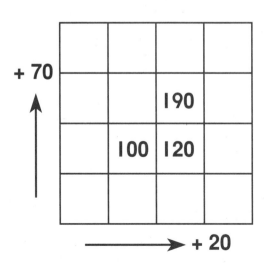

©Addison Wesley Longman, Inc./Published by Dale Seymour Publications®

Geoff bought packages of turkey dogs and buns.

He bought the same number of buns as turkey dogs.

How many packages of turkey dogs did he buy?

How many packages of buns did he buy?

Tell how you know.

- -

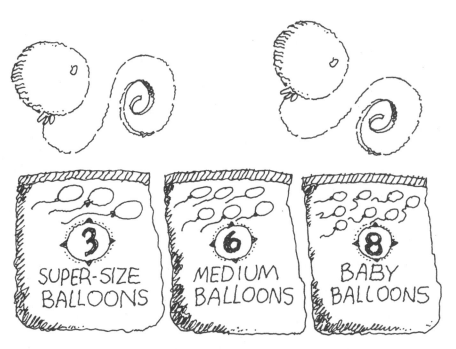

You buy 3 packages of each size balloon.

How many balloons do you buy in all?

Tell two ways to find the answer.

The number 234 has 3 digits.

The sum of the digits is 2 + 3 + 4 = 9.

What other 3-digit numbers less than 300 have digits that add to 9?

Make a list.

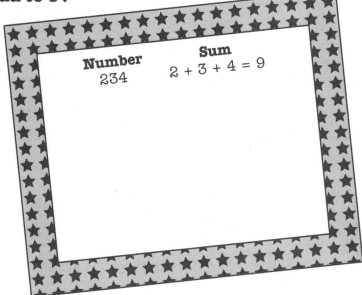

Number	Sum
234	2 + 3 + 4 = 9

©Addison Wesley Longman, Inc./Published by Dale Seymour Publications®

On the left is a magic number wheel.

The sum of the three numbers on each line is 10.

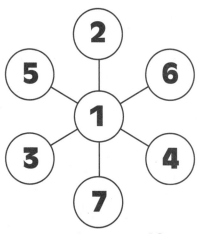

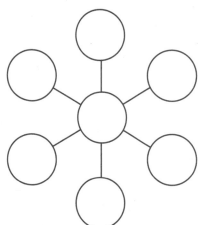

Magic Sum = 10   Magic Sum = 12

Make another magic number wheel.

Put 1, 2, 3, 4, 5, 6, and 7 in the empty circles.

The sum of the three numbers on each line must be 12.

©Addison Wesley Longman, Inc./Published by Dale Seymour Publications®

Get a newspaper.

Write a number from the newspaper that tells you

1. the score of a winning team. _____

2. the date of the newspaper. _____

3. the time of a movie you would like to see. _____

4. yesterday's high temperature. _____

5. the price of something on sale. _____

What else do numbers in the newspaper tell you?

- -

The digits on this digital clock add to 13.

If the digits added to 20, what time could it be?

Make a list of the possible times.

©Addison Wesley Longman, Inc./Published by Dale Seymour Publications®

©Addison Wesley Longman, Inc./Published by Dale Seymour Publications®

You have 1-gram, 5-gram, and 10-gram blocks.

Draw more blocks on the scale to make it balance.

Find another way to balance the scale.

Compare your ways with a classmate's.

- -

Hani bought 10 packs of sports cards.

He bought some 6-card packs.

He bought some 4-card packs.

He bought 54 cards in all.

How many 4-card packs did Hani buy?

©Addison Wesley Longman, Inc./Published by Dale Seymour Publications®

©Addison Wesley Longman, Inc./Published by Dale Seymour Publications®

Fill in the blanks with numbers.

The story must make sense.

Nigel planted tomato plants.

He planted _____ rows of tomato plants.

There were _____ tomato plants in each row.

Each day he weeded _____ rows of tomato plants.

It took Nigel _____ days to weed all his plants.

57

Jin Lee can read about 10 pages in 30 minutes.

At that speed, how many pages can she read in 2 hours?

How do you know?

58

©Addison Wesley Longman, Inc./Published by Dale Seymour Publications®

©Addison Wesley Longman, Inc./Published by Dale Seymour Publications®

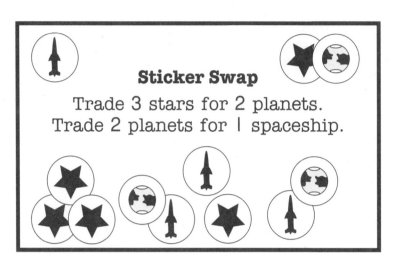

Sticker Swap

Trade 3 stars for 2 planets.
Trade 2 planets for 1 spaceship.

59

You have stickers to trade.

Can you trade for more stars with 4 planets or with 3 spaceships?

Explain.

- -

4 9 6 1

Use all of the digits shown.

Write the greatest 4-digit number.

Use the same digits.

Write the smallest 4-digit number.

Subtract the smallest 4-digit number from the greatest 4 digit number.

What is the difference?

2   1.50   50
5.00   7.00

Use each number shown to complete the story.

Your story must make sense.

Alex bought a sandwich for $ _____ and a glass
of cider for $ _____ .

He gave the clerk $ _____ .

He got _____ quarters, or _____ ¢, in change.

- -

There are 100 jelly beans in jar A.

Estimate the number of jelly beans in jar B.

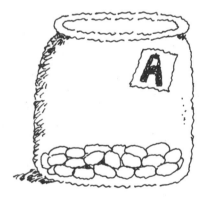

Tell how you decided.

**Compare your estimate with estimates of your
classmates.**

©Addison Wesley Longman, Inc./Published by Dale Seymour Publications®

©Addison Wesley Longman, Inc./Published by Dale Seymour Publications®

Fill in the price tags.

63

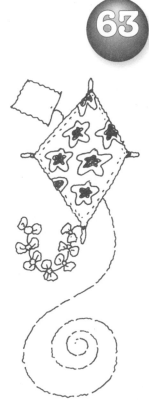

Now use the items and the prices to write 3 problems.

- Write a subtraction problem.
- Write an addition problem.
- Write a problem that uses both addition and subtraction.

Give your problems to a friend to solve.

64

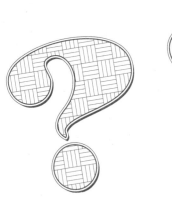  

Manuel is 4 years older than Lee.

Lee is twice as old as Sy.

Sy is 13 years old.

How old is Manuel?

Tell how you figured out his age.

©Addison Wesley Longman, Inc./Published by Dale Seymour Publications®

30   **32**

33   **36**

65

Which of the numbers shown above is the Mystery Number?

- Divide the Mystery Number by 2, and the remainder is 0.

- Divide it by 3, and the remainder is 0.

- Divide it by 4, and the remainder is 0.

- -

66

Use the facts.

Fill in the name of the state next to the population.

State	Population
	550,000
	29,786,000
	11,431,000
	6,016,000
	16,986,000

Facts

- The population of California is about 5 times the population of Massachusetts.

- Texas has about 5 million more people than Illinois has.

- Alaska has less than 1 million people.

©Addison Wesley Longman, Inc./Published by Dale Seymour Publications®

Star City is halfway between Rockettown and Galaxy.

How far is it from Star City to Galaxy?

Tell the steps you used.

- -

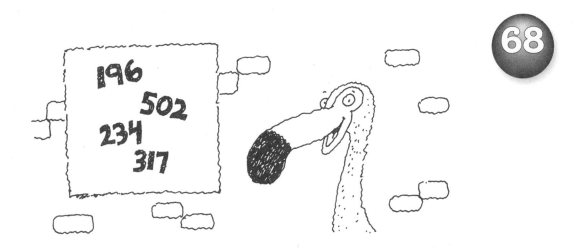

Add 3 numbers on the sign.

How many different sums can you get?

Make a list.

©Addison Wesley Longman, Inc./Published by Dale Seymour Publications®

Jennifer had to find the answer to this
subtraction problem:

$$\begin{array}{r} 400 \\ -\ 199 \\ \hline \end{array}$$

She said, "The answer is the same as the answer
to this problem."

$$\begin{array}{r} 401 \\ -\ 200 \\ \hline \end{array}$$

Is Jennifer right? Explain.

- -

The notebooks are the same.

Which is the better buy, A or B?

Tell why.

©Addison Wesley Longman, Inc./Published by Dale Seymour Publications®

©Addison Wesley Longman, Inc./Published by Dale Seymour Publications®

Fill in each blank with a number.

Your story must make sense.

Paige bought _____ roses for _____ each.

She also bought a ribbon for _____.

Altogether she spent _____.

She gave the clerk _____ and got $.40
in change.

There are 12 children in the play.

- $\frac{1}{2}$ of the children have brown hair.
- $\frac{1}{3}$ of the children have black hair.
- The rest of the children have blond hair.

How many children have blond hair?

Make a drawing to solve the problem.

Find the weight of A and B.

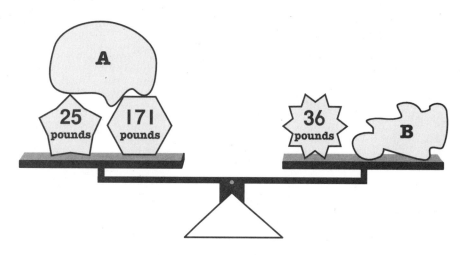

Is there more than one answer?

Explain your thinking.

73

- -

Complete the grid.

Multiply by 5 going across.

Multiply by 2 going up.

74

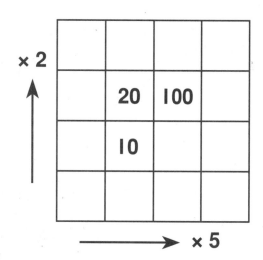

©Addison Wesley Longman, Inc./Published by Dale Seymour Publications®

©Addison Wesley Longman, Inc./Published by Dale Seymour Publications®

©Addison Wesley Longman, Inc./Published by Dale Seymour Publications®

Use a calculator.

What is the greatest 3-digit number you can multiply by 6 and get a product less than 4000?

Now fill in the blanks below with any numbers.

Solve your problem.

What is the greatest 3-digit number you can multiply by _____ and get a product less than _____ ?

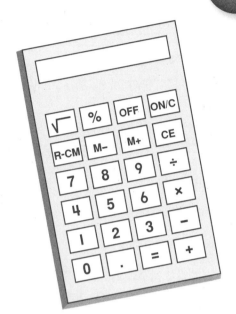

Yvonne has $5.00.

What is the greatest number of markers she can buy?

Name the brand.

Tell how you decided.

Meena bought a sandwich and a drink.

She spent $4.85.

How do you know that she didn't buy a
Very Veggie sandwich?

- -

3¹⁵ **86** **37⁸** **6⁵⁵**

Use the numbers shown.
Estimate to find the answers.

- Which two numbers have a sum of 693?
  _____ and _____

- Which two numbers have a difference of 569?
  _____ and _____

- Which two numbers have a sum greater than
  1000? _____ and _____

- Which two numbers have a difference less
  than 70? _____ and _____

©Addison Wesley Longman, Inc./Published by Dale Seymour Publications®

©Addison Wesley Longman, Inc./Published by Dale Seymour Publications®

Suppose you subtract one 3-digit number from another.

How many digits can there be in the difference?

Give examples.

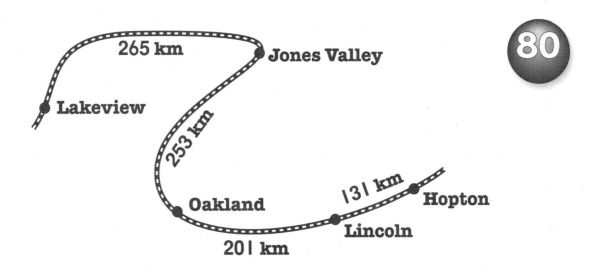

265 km — Jones Valley

Lakeview

253 km

Oakland

131 km — Hopton

Lincoln

201 km

Mr. Choy is driving from Lakeview to Hopton.

He can drive about 720 km on a full tank of gas.

He starts with a full tank.

There is a gas station in each town on the map.

Where do you think he should stop and buy gas? Explain.

81

Kathy bought a fish tank for $24.

She bought a filter that cost half as much as the tank.

She bought 3 fish for $.75 each.

She bought fish food that cost twice as much as one fish.

How much did Kathy spend in all?

- -

82

$$\square + \square + \square = 9$$

$$\square \times \triangle = 18$$

$$\triangle \div \hexagon = \square$$

$$\square = ? \qquad \triangle = ? \qquad \hexagon = ?$$

©Addison Wesley Longman, Inc./Published by Dale Seymour Publications®

©Addison Wesley Longman, Inc./Published by Dale Seymour Publications®

The 6 key on your calculator is broken.

You want to use your calculator to find this sum.

$$739$$
$$+ \; 648$$

What can you do and still use your calculator?
Explain.

- -

How can you use the answer to Problem Y to
solve Problem X?

Problem X	Problem Y
3294	3294
-2197	-2200
	1094

Write a problem that will help you to find the
answer to Problem Z.

Problem Z

$$4958$$
$$-1859$$

©Addison Wesley Longman, Inc./Published by Dale Seymour Publications®

85

Ms. Mercado has $180.

Does she have enough money to buy these four items?

How could you estimate to find the answer?

- -

86

Vlad bought 20 bagels.

He bought plain bagels and sesame bagels.

He bought 3 times as many sesame bagels as plain bagels.

How many plain bagels did Vlad buy?

©Addison Wesley Longman, Inc./Published by Dale Seymour Publications®

Answer Sign

72¢ $3.84

44¢   17¢

87

Use the facts.

Write a question for each answer on the Answer Sign.

Facts

- Taylor bought 6 stickers for 12¢ each.
  She paid with a $1 bill.

- Kyle bought 4 stickers for 29¢ each.
  He paid with a $5 bill.

- -

Which shape has the greater perimeter?

88

a square
whose sides
are each
10 centimeters
long

or

a
triangle
whose sides
are each
2 centimeters
longer than the
square's sides

Explain your answer.

©Addison Wesley Longman, Inc./Published by Dale Seymour Publications®

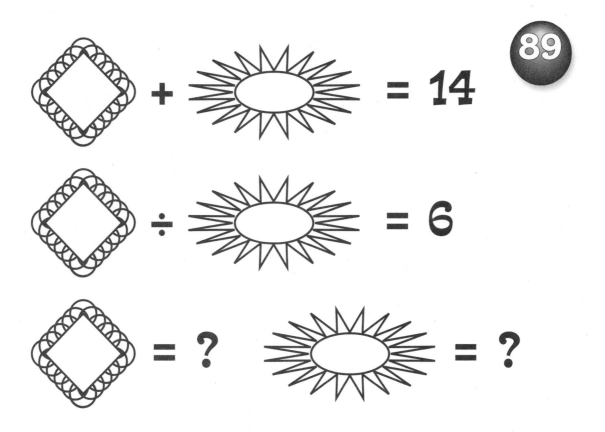

©Addison Wesley Longman, Inc./Published by Dale Seymour Publications®

89

- -

What's the number? ___ ___ , ___ ___ ___

90

Clues

- Use 1, 3, 5, 7, and 9.

- 7 is in the thousands place.

- The number in the hundreds place is 6 more than the number in the ones place.

- The digit in the tens place is less than the digit in the ones place.

Make up a five-digit number. ___ ___ , ___ ___ ___

Write clues to find your number.

Give your problem to a friend to solve.

©Addison Wesley Longman, Inc./Published by Dale Seymour Publications®

Liam bought 3 papayas for $.75 each.

He also bought some bananas that cost $.25 each.

He gave the clerk a $5 bill and got $1.00 change.

How many bananas did Liam buy?

Play with a partner. Use two colors. Take turns.

- Pick a number from A and a number from B.
- Estimate the product.
- Cross out the estimate on the game board.
- The first player with 3 Xs in a row across or down wins.

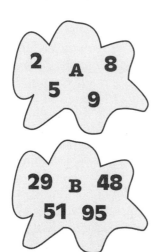

Game Board

250	60	270	100
800	400	240	450
120	540	500	480
150	300	900	200

Get a partner.

Cut out a piece like  .

Put it on the chart.

Have your partner name the covered numbers.

Take turns.

10	20	30	40	50	60	70	80	90	100
110	120	130	140	150	160	170	180	190	200
210	220	230	240	250	260	270	280	290	300
310	320	330	340	350	360	370	380	390	400
410	420	430	440	450	460	470	480	490	500
510	520	530	540	550	560	570	580	590	600
610	620	630	640	650	660	670	680	690	700
710	720	730	740	750	760	770	780	790	800
810	820	830	840	850	860	870	880	890	900
910	920	930	940	950	960	970	980	990	1000

©Addison Wesley Longman, Inc./Published by Dale Seymour Publications®

Which would you rather have?

$\frac{5}{8}$ of the **PIZZA**

$\frac{1}{2}$ of the **PIZZA**

Tell why.

©Addison Wesley Longman, Inc./Published by Dale Seymour Publications®

©Addison Wesley Longman, Inc./Published by Dale Seymour Publications®

| 5 | 2 | 9 | 81 | 35 | 57 |

Use the numbers shown above.

Estimate to decide where to write the numbers.

Use your calculator to check.

 × ⬭ = **513**

□ × ⬭ = **175**

□ × ⬭ = **162**

- -

96

$\frac{1}{2}$  =

$\frac{1}{2}$  = **3**

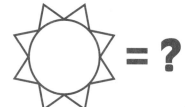 = **?**   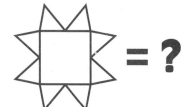 = **?**

Elana made this frame.

How many centimeters of wood did she use?

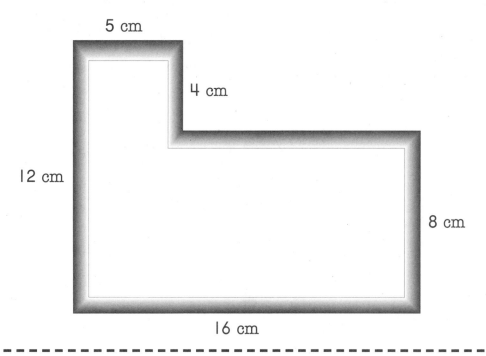

5 cm

4 cm

12 cm

8 cm

16 cm

The price of 4 batteries is the same as the price of 1 calculator.

The price of 1 calculator is $6 more than the price of 1 battery.

Write the prices on the tags.

©Addison Wesley Longman, Inc./Published by Dale Seymour Publications®

©Addison Wesley Longman, Inc./Published by Dale Seymour Publications®

©Addison Wesley Longman, Inc./Published by Dale Seymour Publications®

Chris walked each day for 5 days.

She walked 2 miles on the first day.

Each day she walked 1 more mile than the day before.

After taking her walk on November 3, she had walked a total of 20 miles.

How many miles did she walk that day?

On what date did she start walking?

- -

1 2 3
4 5 6
7 8 9

Use the numbers shown to make the sentences true.

Use each number only once.

_____ + _____ = 10   _____ − _____ − _____ = 0

_____ ÷ _____ = 2   _____ × _____ = 32

Answers

1. $15; Explanations will vary.

2. Mia: a jump rope and a ball; Possible answers for June: a ball, a doll, and crayons *or* 2 jump ropes and a ball *or* 3 dolls; Problems will vary.

3. 52¢; Possible designs: 10 △; 6 △ and 5 □; 2 △ and 10 □

4. 6 caps *or* 2 caps and 3 T-shirts

5. Possible answers: Count the ✿ in a row and multiply by the number of rows. Count the ✿ in a column and multiply by the number of columns.

6. Possible answers:

    • even (0, 2, 4, 6, 8), odd (1, 3, 5, 7, 9)

    • greater than 5 (6, 7, 8, 9), 5 or less (0, 1, 2, 3, 4, 5)

    • numbers you say when counting by 3s (3, 6, 9), numbers you don't say (0, 1, 2, 4, 5, 7, 8)

7. Possible answers:

    • How many or how much: food prices, items in a package

    • Measurements: nutritional information, gas and water meters, thermometers

    • Labels: addresses, TV channel selectors, washing machine dials

8. 93, 96, and 99

9. 24 books; Explanations will vary.

10. Nathan; A total of 23 points is not possible.

11. 21 cookies

12. Answers will vary.

13. Answers will vary.

14. Possible answers: $3 \times 4 + 2 + 1 = 15$; $2 \times (4 + 3) + 1 = 15$; $3 \times (4 + 2 - 1) = 15$

15. 80¢

16. From left to right: Darien, Baytown, Trenton, Sun City, Saugus.

17. Possible answer: How many students are in the two classes altogether? (50) How many more girls than boys are in Everett's class? (6) How many more girls are in Everett's class than in Niki's class? (7) How many boys are in the two classes? (27)

18. A = 34, B = 64, C = 75, D = 86

19. 12, 0; 11, 1; 10, 2; 9, 3; and 8, 4 (Note: Some students may think of negative numbers, such as 15 and −3.)

20. Stories will vary; d

21. 8, 3, 2, 10, 26, 56

22. 5¢ a day for 30 days is $1.50; 10¢ a day for 20 days is $2.00.

23. Answers will vary.

24. 13 and 8; 29 and 32; 59 and 67; 220 and 200

25. 8, 2, 6

26. Lucia: juice, apple; Simon: 2 boxes of raisins, apple

27. No; 9 to the nearest 10 is 10, and 98 to the nearest 10 is 100.

28. Addtown to Divisionville to Multiplicationland to Subtract City

29. State; the city is part of the state. Windows; there are more windows than telephones in a classroom. Thursdays; there are more weeks in a year than days in a month.

30. Answers will vary.

31. 60¢; Possible explanation: 6 pencils is 3 sets of 2 pencils, or 3×20¢, or 60¢. If 2 pencils cost 20¢, one costs 10¢ and 6 cost 6×10¢, or 60¢.

32. 118 miles

```
          35 mi            48 mi
   ●─────────────●──────────────────●
 Upton       Sandhill           Lakeville
```

33. 10; You need 9 boxes for 27 balls and another for the 2 remaining balls.

34. Possible answer: The 2 digits add to 9.

35. The sum in B is 10 more than the sum in A, so the number in the box must be 10 more than 30, or 40.

36. $3.75; Subtract José's total from David's total. Subtract the price of a tie from that of a shirt.

37. 8 tricycles; Explanations will vary.

38. From top to bottom: 6, 18, 2; 7, $\frac{1}{2}$, 4

39. Problems will vary.

40. 1 ball, 1 doll; 1 doll, 1 truck, 1 book; 1 ball, 2 trucks; 1 book, 3 trucks; 1 puzzle, 3 books; 2 puzzles; 6 books

41. 71¢

42. $3.60; Possible answer: Multiply (or add) to find the cost of 4 sets of 3 cookies. Divide to find the cost of 1 cookie and then multiply (or add) to find the cost of 12.

43. one 50¢ and six 1¢; one 25¢, one 10¢, four 5¢, and one 1¢; five 10¢, one 5¢, and one 1¢

44. 8; thick cheese, thin cheese, thick pepperoni, thin pepperoni, thick onion, thin onion, thick garlic, thin garlic

45. 2, 4, 9 balances 3, 5, 7

46. $2.40; She paid for 4 cans: 4×60¢ = $2.40.

47. 48

48.

220	240	260	280
150	170	190	210
80	100	120	140
10	30	50	70

49. Possible answers: 3 packages of turkey dogs and 4 of buns, 6 packages of dogs and 8 of buns, and so on; Explanations will vary.

50. 51 balloons; Possible answer: Find the total number of balloons when you buy one package of each, $3 + 6 + 8 = 17$, and multiply by 3, $17 \times 3 = 51$. Multiply the number of balloons in each package by 3 and then add: $9 + 18 + 24 = 51$.

51. 108, 117, 126, 135, 144, 153, 162, 171, 180, 207, 216, 225, 243, 252, 261, 270

52. Possible answer:

53. Numbers will vary. Possible answers: page numbers, facts in articles, TV times, other sports statistics, addresses

54. 6:59, 7:49, 7:58, 8:39, 8:48, 8:57, 9:38, 9:47, 9:56

55. Answers will vary.

56. 3 four-card packs

57. Answers will vary.

58. 40 pages; Possible explanation: 2 hours is four 30-minute periods, for $4 \times 10 = 40$ pages.

59. 3 spaceships; Possible explanation: 4 planets trade for 6 stars; 3 spaceships trade for 6 planets, which trade for 9 stars.

60. $9641 - 1469 = 8172$

61. 5.00, 1.50, 7.00, 2, 50

62. about 500 jelly beans; Possible explanation: About 5 times as many jelly beans are in jar B as jar A.

63. Answers will vary.

64. 30 years old; Lee is $2 \times 13 = 26$, so Manuel is $26 + 4 = 30$.

65. 36

66. Alaska, California, Illinois, Massachusetts, Texas

67. 25 km; It is $90 - 40 = 50$ km from Rockettown to Galaxy, so it is $50 \div 2 = 25$ km from Star City to Galaxy.

68. 747, 932, 1015, 1053

69. yes; 401 is 1 more than 400, and 200 is 1 more than 199, so the differences will be the same.

70. A; Possible explanation: 2 A notebooks cost about $2.00, so 1 A is about $1.00. If each B notebook were about $1.00, 3 B notebooks would be about $3.00, not $4.00.

71. Answers will vary.

72. 2 children; Possible drawing:

brown   black   blond

73. Answers will vary. Any pair of numbers will work as long as B is 160 lb more than A.

74.

8	40	200	1000
4	20	100	500
2	10	50	250
1	5	25	125

75. 666; Problems will vary.

76. 15 markers; Rainbow; Possible explanation: Each set of 3 Rainbow markers costs about $1.00, so for $5.00 she could buy 15 markers.

77. Possible answer: Meena would have had $4.85 - $4.15 = $.70 left over, and a drink costs at least $1.00.

78. 315 and 378; 655 and 86; 378 and 655; 378 and 315

79. 1, 2, or 3 digits; Possible examples: $302 - 298 = 4$; $200 - 175 = 25$; $485 - 122 = 363$

80. It is 719 km from Lakeview to Lincoln. Since 720 is an estimate, it is best to buy gas in Oakland.

81. $39.75

82. 3, 6, 2

83. Answers will vary.

84. Add 3 to 1094 to get 1097. Problems will vary.

85. Possible answer: Round each price up to the nearest $10: $80 + 30 + 50 + 20 = \$180$. Since each number was rounded up, she has enough.

86. 5 plain bagels

87. Possible answer: How much did Taylor spend? (72¢) How much change did Kyle receive? ($3.84) How much more did Kyle spend than Taylor? (44¢) How much more did one of Kyle's stickers cost than one of Taylor's? (17¢)

88. the square; perimeter of square $= 4 \times 10 = 40$ cm, perimeter of triangle $= 3 \times 12 = 36$ cm

89. 12, 2

90. 57,913; Numbers and clues will vary.

91. 7 bananas

94. If students want more pizza, $\frac{5}{8}$ of a pizza; Students may make diagrams or rewrite the fractions: $\frac{5}{8} > \frac{4}{8}$.

95. $9 \times 57 = 513$, $5 \times 35 = 175$, $2 \times 81 = 162$

96. 6, 12

97. about 56 cm

98. battery, $2; calculator, $8

99. 6 miles, October 30

100. $9 + 1 = 10$, $4 \times 8 = 32$, $6 \div 3 = 2$, $7 - 5 - 2 = 0$